The Power Within
Claiming Your Personal Power

By Alise Spiritual Healing & Wellness Center

This book may be ordered through booksellers or by contacting:

iGlobal Educational Services, LLC
13785 Highway 183, Suite 125
Austin, Texas 78750
www.iglobaleducation.com
512-761-5898

Because of the dynamic nature of the Internet, any web addresses or links contained in this book may have changed since publication and may no longer be valid. The views expressed in this work are solely those of the author and do not necessarily reflect the views of the publisher, and the publisher hereby disclaims any responsibility for them.

This is a work of fiction. Names, characters, businesses, places, events, and incidents are either the products of the author's imagination or used in a fictitious manner. Any resemblance to actual persons, living or dead, or actual events is purely coincidental.

The Power Within: Claiming Your Personal Power

ISBN-13: 978-1-944346-31-7

Dedication

This book is dedicated to all the courageous beings who are stepping out on faith to claim their personal power. You are never alone on this spiritual journey. Know that you are loved, you are valued, and you are competent.

ACKNOWLEDGMENTS

I cannot say this enough, but I must give glory to God for helping me realize my potential and purpose in life. It was He whom brought Natasa and Jasmine together to manifest this project. There are truly no words to express my gratitude as each of you are truly a blessing to our healing center.

I also want to thank Surendra Gupta for his creativity in formatting and Pankaj Singh Renu for his creativity in designing our book. Both of you are amazing!

Table of Contents

Chapter 1
The Power of
Vision Boards

A clever, well-crafted vision is the key driving force of life. Without it, all the labor, sincerity and intent you invest in anything you do will be without fruition.

This basic fact is the reason behind such an astounding success of vision boards.

Vision boards are the leading tool for maintaining motivation and achieving personal goals. This new-age miracle will transform your life, enabling you to focus on taking action and fulfilling your wildest dreams.

Sounds great, doesn't it?

Let's take a closer look at what vision boards are and how they work. You'll be surprised with how easy it is to create and use this amazing tool.

The Basics

Let's first understand what a vision board is. It is primarily a physical picture or a compilation of pictures that depicts an individual's vision for his own future. It allows you to focus on attainable goals by making them concrete.

Clipping a picture on a vision board does several things:

1. It makes your goals tangible, clear and specific.

2. It gives you something to focus on as you collect new achievements.

3. It reminds you of your dreams, as they are in your constant view.

Creating Online Vision Boards

Did you know that you could create your own vision board online? Some people may call it a collage, but it works just like a vision board. The concept works the same way, but it may actually take less time to create and you will have an opportunity to change out the vision board quite often. Let's look at a few of our clients' stories regarding their own vision boards:

Scenario: "My Car is Coming to Me"

Diamond, a single mom, has been driving an old white car. Week after week, there was something wrong with the car. It got so bad that she had to put power steering fluids in her car on a daily basis to even turn the wheel. One day, after seeing an online ad for a Vision Board Workshop hosted by Minister Alise, she decided to enroll and take the class. The class was held at a local hotel and had about 10 participants. Diamond partnered up with another lady named Sophia. They both created their own physical vision boards. Their main theme was to feel empowered. Sophia, a single

---

mom as well, needed a better car to get to her job and take her kids to school. On their vision board, they put the specific car brand that they desired, along with the color of the car. Diamond also added that she desired a "Godly Man", more clients for her business, and a trip to Jamaica. Sophia desired a house of her own and a vacation for her family. She and her family had not taken a vacation in more than four years after the divorce from her ex-husband. About three months later, Diamond emailed and shared with Minister Alise that she had got her car—the one that she had on her vision board. Shortly after, Sophia also called and shared that she had been approved for a car loan to get the dream car for her family.

1. How do you plan on creating your vision board? Will it be a physical or online vision board?

_____

_____

_____

_____

_____

_____

_____

_____

2. What are the desires of your heart that you would like to manifest?

_____

_____

_____

_____

_____

_____

_____

3. What are you willing to do to help manifest these desires that you will place on your vision board?

_____

_____

_____

_____

_____

_____

_____

4. *Do you plan on keeping a journal to document your experiences? Why or why not?*

_____

_____

_____

_____

_____

_____

_____

The Amazing Power of Vision Boards

The logic behind a vision board lies in the core concept of visualization.

Visualization is the art of using mental imagery to create visions of your aspirations. Through it, you will create virtual images of your goals and wishes in life.

When you create a vision board, these mental images are translated onto a physical board, bringing the power of visualization to life.

Simply put, vision boards intensify the power of visualization by being a pillar that supports your dreams at all times.

The Elusive Law of Attraction

The always present (but seldom felt) law of attraction is the second most important logic behind the vision boards.

This powerful natural law is based on the simple principle of positivity. A positive attitude will always attract positivity in your life, and vice versa. Furthermore, the premise of the law of attraction explains that positive thinking and an optimistic outlook pave the way for success even in adverse circumstances.

Once you pin your desired goals and aspirations onto the vision board in the form of real pictures, it starts attracting positivity into your life. Both your mind and body start to work together, striving to bring those images and visions to real life.

Try this...

The best way to prove how well visual boards work is personal experience. But, let's use an example, as it can help with understanding just how amazing this concept is.

Imagine that you are a mother or father of a growing adolescent. You aspire for a bright professional career for your child. You do your research and you find images of the places where you'd like him/her to study or work. Put these up on your vision board, where you can see them and use the laws described in this chapter to bring your dreams to life.

While things might not fall exactly in line with the pictures, the Spirit will find a way to bring your aspirations to fruition, as long as you have the right direction.

From here on, we'll start revealing the connection between dreams and achievements, and how they relate to vision boards.

Chapter 2
Your Goals and Dreams

Have you ever thought about what keeps you away from that elusive achievement, success or happiness? Just have another look at your goals and objectives for a moment.

When it comes to achieving goals, dreams are the basic element in every word of advice. Whether in religious scripts or the famous talks by any success coach across the world, dreams are the core concept, the seed from which success grows to life.

Let's take a closer look at how significant your dreams and goals can be in giving you the life you ideally want.

Dreams – the First Baby Steps

Everything begins with a dream. While some dismiss the tiny vision as just a simple whim, others clutch their dream. It is here that you begin to nurture your thought, your vision, like a sapling. After all, it has never hurt anyone to let their imagination simply flow.

Here, it also helps to know from where your dreams emanate. Our mind works at two different levels, the conscious and the subconscious mind. Isn't it surprising how oblivious we are to our subconscious mind, which is the driving force of the conscious self? All our thoughts, aspirations and feelings are stored deep inside our subconscious mind. It is these sensations that come to life in our dreams and visions, nudging us to act in life.

Fascinating, isn't it?

Now, let's take some time to write down some of your dreams.

Self-Reflection: Connecting with Your Dreams

1. *As a child, what did you always dream of becoming or doing in your life? Please be specific to help you see the connection between your dreams and goals.*

_____

_____

_____

_____

_____

_____

_____

_____

_____

_____

Let's move ahead to the next milestone of translating your dream to a concrete, result-oriented goal.

Goals – the Road to Success

Ironic as it might sound, it is at this stage where most of us falter. If you fail to turn your dream or vision into a specific goal, you will only be left with a mass of frustration and uncertainty in life.

First of all, it is important that you know what you really want in life. Once you figure that out, you need to make a list of concrete steps towards accomplishing your objectives.

For instance, if you aspire to increase your fortune, you first need to analyze your current income and expenditure patterns. You then need to research your investment options, and in the end decide on the funds you need to achieve your ultimate goal.

So, let's take a look at a process that can help you set some SMART goals, in which SMART stands for **S**pecific, **M**easurable, **A**chievable, **R**ealistic, and **T**imely.

When you are writing your own SMART goals, you may decide to choose some of the alternative adjectives.

Here's some helpful tips to better help you understand how to write your goals:

- **S** - specific, significant, stretching
- **M** - measurable, meaningful, motivational
- **A** - agreed upon, attainable, achievable, acceptable, action-oriented
- **R** - realistic, relevant, reasonable, rewarding, results-oriented
- **T** - time-based, timely, tangible, trackable

Below is an example:

An Example for You

I will write a book series about my life by the end of 2016.

With this major goal in mind, you need to focus on at least 1-3 minor goals that you would like to accomplish.

Are you ready? Now, it's time to take what you have learned about SMART goals and write your own. Please use the space below to write your goals.

Goal # 1

S - _____

M - _____

A - _____

R- _____

T - _____

Goal # 2

S - _____

M - _____

A - _____

R- _____

T -

```
Goal # 3
S - _____
M - _____
A - _____
R- _____
T - 
```

A Word of Advice

Life and success are delicate matters of mind, body and soul. It takes an intricate connection of visions, dreams, goals and objectives to make your life the way you want it to be. Just take baby steps and watch them all roll into a big success story!

Chapter 3
Your First Steps to
Positive Intentions

The human mind only thrives in a positive ambience. Such is the nature of this world that anyone with a pessimistic or negative approach will simply attract negativity, bringing confusion into their lives.

So, let us show you how to go about building a world of optimism and positive intentions for yourself.

You'll be surprised at how easy it is... Everyone can do it with just a bit of effort!

Have a Taste for Life

As you see, it is a journey backwards. Once you have a taste for living a good life, you will strive to achieve anything that will bring that life closer to you. It is true that money doesn't buy happiness, but you definitely need resources to fulfill your aspirations.

Once you know what it takes to build the life you want, your brain will work to build a positive environment in your subconscious mind. The reason for this lies in the simple fact that no achievement in the world is possible unless you bear a positive outlook and a will to achieve.

Choose Your Environment

When you set out to build positive intentions for yourself, choose the people and places around you carefully. It may surprise you to know how much the people around you can have an impact on your mental make-up. While the positive-minded people will help you look ahead and achieve your dreams, those with a negative attitude will pull you back.

Sounds familiar? How many times did you feel down only because someone else was forcing these negative mind states on you?

What's more, their negative actions, such as lamenting on how bad the world is, how difficult your task is, and similar, will influence your reality in a very negative way.

Even if you cannot break contact with such people (because some bonds are very difficult to let go of, even when the differences are too big), try not to let their outlook wash over you.

Know what Boosts You

A morning cup of hot tea while reading the newspaper might boost some, just like a brisk jog might lift someone else's spirits. Know what puts you in the right frame of mind. Learn to do this as a part of your daily routine. Do not wait for a crisis to put your positive gears into action.

Make sure to keep your habits healthy. A healthy body is home to a healthy spirit.

Just a Thought

Life is full of both sorrowful disappointments and pleasant surprises. Keep your mental metabolism in balance with a strong armor of positive intentions. This is imperative if you wish to live a fulfilled life, unaffected by the sudden twists and turns the journey might have to offer.

Chapter 4
Belief Systems as Lighthouses

Think about it for a moment – the entire humanity shares the same world, the same cosmos, with a unified guiding force behind us. Yet, each of us comes with a different set of thoughts, perceptions, ideologies and countless other items as baggage.

Like a hiker who bundles up his essential supplies in a rucksack, we pack ourselves with scores of such principles and thoughts that eventually become our guiding source of life. This web of thoughts, attitudes and opinions is exactly what we casually call our belief system.

A belief system is your inner driving force. It governs how you deal with problems and receive happiness in life. It also governs how you manage the sensitive relationships in your life. In other words, it works as a lighthouse to illuminate your path ahead.

In his book, "I am Worthy", the Businessman, Inspirational Speaker, and Author, Chris Grant, shares how the link of belief systems and one's thoughts shape how he or she will engage in daily life activities. His non-profit, King Salute Foundation, is dedicated to bringing out the best in everyone, and he speaks regularly on belief systems, shaping one's thoughts, and living out one's God-Given Destiny. Please check our website to see when he is near your city as he travels the world sharing the message that you are **loved**, you are **valued**, and you are **competent**. If you would like for him to come and speak at your organization, please contact us here at the Alise Spiritual Healing & Wellness Center.

The Inheritance

We are all born with unique DNA in our body. Our genetic mapping is different, and so is our physical appearance. Along with this, we are also born with a few mindsets and ideologies, which somehow seem to be a part of our belief system.

For instance, your family might not do any charity outside home, but goes to any extent to help its own staff when required. This will gradually teach the kids in the family that charity begins at home and no display of philanthropy is required.

What is important is to respect your own inherited beliefs and values. Respect them as a part of your personality and be proud of your values. Know that the Spirit wanted you to live with these principles.

The Acquired Perceptions

We tend to acquire a huge range of ideas, opinions and perceptions as we move and mingle with the outer world. The irony here is that not all inputs from the people around you are desirable. You need to have the sensibility to separate the wheat from the chaff so that you keep your psychological health clean.

To be able to do the above, you need to have your inherited belief system in place, like a sound base to build a house on. Your internal mechanism should be strong and mature enough to recognize the harmful influences around you. You then need to ward away the beliefs that do not suit your original self. Do this with a lot of care and sensitivity to avoid hurting the feelings of those around you.

Chapter 5
Why Visualization is Important

A rocket is often used to send men or technology into space. However, it will only be able to fulfill its purpose if it is fired in the right direction. An aimless rocket will not only leave the objective unsolved; it will also end up causing unnecessary damage where it is not required.

Energy, willpower and hard work without a concrete vision are bound to do just the same. Like a misfired, aimless rocket can be hazardous, hard work without a vision can cause immense frustration and disappointment in life.

Visualization is an art of being able to put your future aims into concrete mental images. We use imagery to gain concentration and provide relaxation in life.

Let us look at the two key reasons why visualization is such an important part of our result-oriented lives.

Workers – the Novice and the Amateur

There are two types of people in the world. The first category is the novice workers: those that are still deciding on their course in life. Their current situation of not knowing their path in life could either be because of their age, or a consequence of a lack of focus.

For such individuals, visualization is the last straw they can hold on to. They need to develop a complete vision of what they want in life so that they can work to achieve their milestones.

Let's look at Maggie—**Novice**.

Scenario: I'm Going for Mine

Maggie got her first job at a local retail supercenter. She started working in the jewelry department, and actually enjoyed her job. She met a guy one day while at work and he asked her out. His name was Curt. After two dates, Curt and Maggie started dating. She was getting paid weekly, but she was not paying her bills. Instead, she was paying Curt's bills. Maggie got a notice to vacate her apartment due to non-payment. She asked Curt to help pay her rent and he told her that he did not have any money to help her. That's when Maggie saw an online add about life coaching. She called the life coaching center and scheduled her an appointment to help her through the next steps.

If you were Maggie's Life Coach, what would you say to help her? How could you help Maggie turn her life around?

_____

_____

_____

_____

_____

_____

_____

_____

_____

The amateurs are those who are well ahead on their path of life fall into the next category. They are already on their desired paths and have a vision to follow.

Individuals in this category require strong visualizing techniques to keep themselves focused and on track to achieve their present goals. Any deviations could prove harmful to the potential success.

Let's look at Kingston Green—**Amateur**.

Scenario: I Walk with the Spirit

Kingston has recently taken more time out for a relationship with the Spirit. He is of Christian Faith so he calls the Spirit God, Holy Spirit, Jesus. He spends several hours in devotion to receive his message for the day, and learn how to proceed. He does not act on emotions, but rather takes steps back to make a solid decision. He makes decisions from the heart, rather than from the flesh. He has full self-control and is still working on learning how to use his head. He realizes that he is not perfect, but needs a support system to help him reach his full potential. He now understands the purpose of dating, and how significant it is to marry the right woman. A woman that is virtuous and knows her role as a partner, mother, and wife. He is learning that it is all about the energy rather than physical beauty. Inner beauty is what truly matters. It's the true essence of the soul and the life force of humanity.

If you were Kingston's Life Coach, what would you say to help him? How could you help Kingston turn his life around?

_____

_____

_____

_____

_____

_____

_____

_____

_____

_____

_____

Have you ever had a life coach? If so, what was your experience with them?

_____

_____

_____

_____

_____

_____

_____

_____

_____

_____

_____

If you are looking for a life coach, let the Alise Spiritual Healing & Wellness Center find you one that would be a good match to work with you.

The Distraction Advantage

Visualization, in the form of mental imagery, also offers you a major tool for relaxation and enhancement of your concentration levels. This is a technique in which you hoard soothing images in your mind, so that you can think of them when under stress. Simply visualizing these images relieves you of anxiety and rejuvenates your whole self.

Having trouble with stressful situations?

Let's say you're invited to an interview for the job of your dreams. You know in your heart that you're a great candidate. You have the needed experience and expertise.

But you can't help being nervous. Your gut twists in anticipation of the interview, and try as you may, you can't keep your thoughts in order.

So what do you do? Do you let your anxiety take control of you? Do you let it show in the interview that could change your life, by stuttering, sweating, or getting confused?

Of course not!

You will summon the images you put on your vision board. Think of that gorgeous snowy landscape, peaceful, glowing under the bright sun. Think of that beach you pinned, its clear water gently brushing against the golden grains of the sand.

Let the waves wash over your worries. Feel your toes dip into that sand. Connect to the Earth, to the Spirit. You are strong, bold, as a ship braving the storm somewhere on the distant horizon. Your abilities stretch as far and deep as that sapphire-blue sky above you.

You have nothing to fear.

Put simply, visualization is a powerful psychological tool that can help you succeed in life. It helps you to move a couple of steps ahead of yourself. It shows you the path, which synchronizes with your original goals in life.

It is clear from that why vision boards are the most amazing tool for visualization, and therefore, taking action.

Chapter 6
Meditation and Mindfulness

We, the human beings, have a tendency to be more in the repair mode than in the prevention stage, at least most of the time. We often tend to take liberties with our mental and physical selves, disregarding the potential consequences of our actions.

After all, how often is it that we recognize the symptoms of stress and fatigue, which our mind and body emit so frequently? Do we ever slow down and let our senses repair? Instead, we just forge ahead in our worldly pursuits.

It is for this reason that the ancient art of meditation has the most relevance for the busy and stressed out man of today. Within meditation, it is mindfulness which takes the center stage, since it helps you focus on a single point in your mind.

There are so many different types of meditation and mindfulness strategies, so you can easily try to find the one that will benefit

you on a daily basis. Let's take a look at the some types of meditations which you can introduce into your daily life:

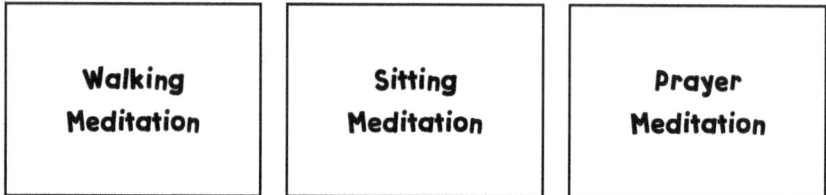

Walking Meditation	Sitting Meditation	Prayer Meditation

Walking Meditation

Walking meditation, as its name says, uses the walking experience
as a way to focus. You observe your surroundings while walking,
taking in everything in your environment, keeping your awareness
level high.

Take a deep breath, then start walking at a normal pace. As you
walk, feel the air flow, hear the sounds of nature, or the sounds of
a bustling city, depending on where you are. Feel the earth under
your feet, and with each step, feel the difference your movement
makes in the environment. Take everything in. As you move, you
will become increasingly aware of your own body, and experi-
encing the outside world will help you get in touch with your
inner self.

It is common knowledge that walking is very beneficial for your
health. By practicing the walking meditation, not only do you
improve your health, but you walk a spiritual path, too.

If you're not comfortable enough with the city traffic, try searching for a park, or an oasis in nature for your first attempts at the
walking meditation.

Sitting Meditation

The most commonly known kind of meditation is the sitting meditation. You settle in a comfortable position, keeping your spine straight, your chin pulled back, and your lower body comfortable as you let the energy flow through your chakras.

It's important to stay comfortable, as meditating in a sitting position can prove challenging for the inexperienced. Be mindful of the factors that may make this kind of meditation difficult, such as the room temperature, having your stomach full, outside noise and other distractions.

Take deep, slow breaths. With each breath, you form a connection to the Spirit. With your lower chakras, you become deeply rooted, while the upper allow you to reach out to the Heavens, to the Universe. Becoming one with the world, you enrich your humanity with the Divine.

Sitting meditation is healthy for the spirit, because it provides uninterrupted energy flow down your spine, which moves to the other sections of your body, healing you, while your mind reaches for the full awareness.

It can be a humbling, deeply moving experience.

Prayer Meditation

Prayer meditation is a form of reflecting upon the revelations directed from the Spirit, where you became aware of His intentions for you. You retain your focus on a specific thought, a question, or a religious passage, and reflect on it, keeping the Universal nature of the Spirit's love in mind.

By practicing the prayer meditation, the personal relationship between you and the Spirit springs and grows into a beautiful tree, connecting you to the Divine. This tree is as healthy as your thoughts are clear, with your faith like water, giving it life, and your hope like the Sun, keeping it strong.

Prayer meditation is more structured and concise than a regular prayer, and though it serves a similar purpose, it provides a stronger link to the Spirit by searching for the answers from inside you.

As you meditate, you allow the Spirit to enter your soul, providing a better understanding of the theme of your prayer as you ponder its message.

These are just three types of meditations that can help you throughout your daily life.

As you are using these meditations, it is extremely important to journal your experiences and reflect upon them. If you are not able to do this on a daily basis, then just jot down the biggest 'aha' moments so that you can begin to see a pattern of any changes in your thought patterns, behaviors, and choices. Most importantly, you should document your ability to focus and be mindful of our choices.

Keeping Your Journal: What You Need to Include In It

A journal is your best friend when you are trying to practice meditation and just grow in all areas of your life. If you do not feel comfortable writing in a journal, then you can record an audio post about your meditation experiences or record a video.

Whatever you decide to do, you need to make sure that you include some key information.

Self-Reflection: Connecting with Your Meditations

1. *What insights did you have as you meditated? Please be specific and feel free to summarize your insights for one day or multiple days to see a pattern.*

_____

_____

_____

_____

_____

_____

_____

_____

_____

_____

_____

_____

_____

_____

_____

_____

_____

_____

_____

_____

_____

_____

_____

_____

_____

_____

_____

_____

_____

_____

Here's how you can introduce meditation into your daily life, with a special focus on mindfulness, and let it enrich your existence.

Mindfulness

Do we really know what meditation and mindfulness are all about, and how exactly each of these can help us when used alongside vision boards?

When you meditate, you basically learn to focus on the core of your existence and get in touch with your inner self. The main benefits of meditation are relaxation and improvement in concentration.

Mindfulness takes you a step further and helps you focus on the epicenter of your thought process, whether it involves a situation, a problem, or an individual. It helps you divert all your energies towards the present moment, so that you can pay attention to a single aspect in your life.

Eventually, you end up in a state of mind where you can simply focus on the issue or thought at hand, without allowing any other feeling to disturb your concentration.

Once you've understood how useful meditation and mindfulness are to you, you then need to look into what the best course of action for your situation is. To begin, it is important that you start using the core breathing exercises, as a part of whole-body meditation.

With help from your spiritual guru, learn to focus on your breathing patterns. This will help you regain your composure, and it will give you some relief from stress.

Why It Works

So what is it that makes meditation and mindfulness work? Since the human mind is full of conflicting thoughts and emotions, it is often very difficult to focus and stay calm. Such practices help you regain your focus in life and concentrate on the present moment, teaching you how to react to distractions around you.

Meditation basically makes the brain waves move from a higher to lower frequency, which brings you closer to inner peace. As your thoughts become slower, you'll find it easier to process them, and to look at things from a different angle. This new perspective helps you reach the state of awareness necessary to connect with the nature of the world, as it is intended for you as a spiritual being.

The modern life is fast, too fast for the gentle nature of our souls. As we are forced to deal with the difficulties in our daily lives, meditation and mindfulness help us slow down and explore our problems with the newly found information from the other side of the spectrum of human life.

In the following chapters, we'll go through another powerful tool that will change your life for the better – and you'll be surprised to see for yourself what a simple, yet wonderful tool it is!

Chapter 7
Affirmations: The Anchors of Your Life

The best of ships need anchors and lighthouses to sail through their journey. Even the most determined souls and focused individuals tend to lose focus in the maze of life.

Our ancestors were major survivors, going only by their instinct and the will to live through the odds. As time progressed, man had to face more of unknown pressures and challenges. This actually threatened his survivor instinct, giving birth to such support systems like affirmations. What the ancient man had known all along, the modern man calls by a different name! Affirmations have been around for such a long time. Who would have known?

What are Affirmations?

Affirmations are a cluster of self-regulating action points that help you stay focused on your goals in life. Affirmations are usually written in the form of short, powerful statements, and they reinforce your belief in your goals.

Below are some affirmations that you can use in your own life:

Positive Affirmations for Gratitude

1. I am so grateful for the supportive family and friends I have.
2. The Spirit is my provider and I have everything I need. My heart is open to more of what the Spirit has in store for me.
3. Life is beautiful and I am blessed to be so lucky.
4. I am blessed to have good health, a lovely family and a great profession.
5. I am grateful for the abundant blessing of strength to overcome all my difficulties in life.
6. I show gratitude for all the joy in my life with every step I take.

Positive Affirmations for Self-Confidence

1. Every day is a better day.
2. The Spirit watches over me and He will take care of me.
3. I have a good decision making power.
4. I can achieve what I want to with my own efforts.
5. I keep my focus firm, and solve my problems with a clear mind.
6. I meet the challenges in my life with confidence and greatness of spirit.

Positive Affirmations for Success

1. I have full faith in the Spirit's mysterious ways.
2. The world is turning better every day, and everything goes in my favor.
3. I attract success with every breath I take.
4. I utilize every opportunity presented to me with the best of my efforts.
5. I reach out to the power within me to help me win.
6. I am a winner. With hard work, I conquer.

Positive Affirmations for Self-Love

1. I am loved, I am valued, and I am competent.
2. I am here for a unique purpose, only I can fulfill.
3. I have a strong, powerful and positive mind that is my best friend.
4. I accept myself as a unique, special person worthy of love and respect.
5. I am healthy, positive and powerful, facing the world with the best of my abilities.
6. I live my life to the fullest, achieving anything I imagine.

Now, let's take a look at how your brain works and how that is related to affirmations.

Know Your Brain – the Reticular Activating System

The purpose and role of affirmations is to unlock the potential of your built-in Reticular Activating System (RAS). This is an actual mechanism in our brain that helps filter the relevant and useful thoughts from all that you see, think and feel in your waking hours.

Once you have made an affirmation, your RAS takes it as a signal and assimilates all that is relevant to help you achieve your goal.

For instance, your goal is to improve your professional career. You will begin by believing that you are already on the way to achieve a better job, through powerful positive affirmations made to yourself before going to bed every night.

Once that's done, your RAS will get activated and will begin to look for options to help you achieve your goal. As if on a cue, new investment and placement options will get your attention.

The Menace of Distraction

Another purpose of affirmations is warding off distractions and helping you stay on track. You are commonly facing scores of distractions in your daily life. This can hamper the progress towards your goals!

When you use vision boards and you write your affirmations repeatedly, these tools help you stay focused on your specific objective. It is a scientifically proven fact that the brain benefits from repetition and pointers such as these.

Spiritual and commercial success often comes hard in life. It is important that you use as many anchors and tools as you can for support, affirmations being a major one amongst these.

The Three Steps to Amazing, Powerful and Positive Affirmations

Practice and knowledge see you through the worst of challenges. Nothing can be harder than overcoming your inner demons of negativity and self-doubt in life.

With a little insight and the right perspective, you can excel at the art of writing powerful, positive affirmations that work, in the following three easy-to-follow steps.

The Three-Step Wonder

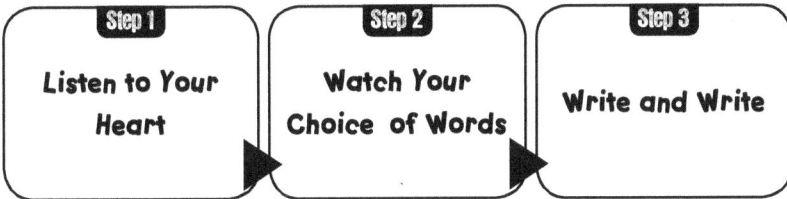

Step 1	Step 2	Step 3
Listen to Your Heart	Watch Your Choice of Words	Write and Write

Listen to Your Heart

Whatever your goal in life may be, your mind and heart will always be your best friend. While your mind helps you think straight, your heart tells you what you really want. The first step to writing powerful affirmations is to listen to your heart and write what it tells you to. Grab the thought and just write it without giving a second thought, even if it sounds very immature.

Be your unique self and see your thoughts unroll.

Watch your choice of Words

Stay away from negative words. Choose words that emit positivity. For instance, stay away from words like avoid, hate, lonely, sad, fear etc. You will actually be surprised to know how you'll be able to say the same thing using positive words such as like, love, hope, prefer, lucky, blessed and so on.

Use the litmus test for your affirmations. Using a litmus test means that you test something to see if it's acceptable, and this is how you do it: speak the affirmation loudly, to yourself, after you have written it. If the immediate feel is negative, discard it right away. Here's an example:

Let's say that you want to use a self-empowering affirmation, and you start searching for the "right one". You decide to try this one: *I am filled with happiness in my life, I reject misery and negativity.*

Everything seems right at first. However, as you continue writing your affirmation down and pondering on its deeper meaning, you notice that its effects are weaker. Maybe you notice some negative thoughts and emotions. Maybe there's sadness.

So what went wrong?

Remember that words are powerful. Even when you said that you reject misery and negativity, you still used these words, and by doing so you gave them power to enter your life.

Negativity is like a leech sinking into your spirit where you're the most vulnerable. Until you are ready to focus power into your words, use only positive ones. You do not want to affirm negative constructions or wishful thinking, like for example "I want to be happy." Instead, use a simple, positive sentence: *I am filled with happiness in my life. I am grateful for all the good things life has provided me with. I am healthy. I am humble. I am strong. I am beautiful.*

Write and Write

Write down the affirmation or thought immediately. Never assume that you remember it by heart. Writing it down consolidates the thought in your mind. For best usage, maintain a journal in which you write down the affirmation with the time and date. This will help you recollect how you felt on a certain day and help you gain more positivity in times of shortage.

But what happens if a good idea for an affirmation comes to you when you least expect it?

Do not underestimate the power of your subconscious. It might just send you the thoughts that would work as great affirmations. Such is the nature of our inner self that it strives to bring out the best in us, so it often works on its own, while we're sleeping, working, or are otherwise busy.

This is why it is a good idea to keep a small, handy notebook in your purse, in your car, in your office, even in your kitchen! You can use these to write your ideas down, and then you can easily pin them to your vision board or re-write them in a special journal.

A good idea is to keep a stack of post-it notes near you, so you can write your affirmations on bright, colorful paper and place them somewhere where you'll be able to see them at all times.

As you re-write and re-read your affirmations, you'll naturally plant them into your subconscious, and you'll start seeing the results of your efforts.

Chapter 8
Affirmations and Meditations: A Powerful Combination

A peaceful mind is home to the finest of thoughts and visions, and limitless inner strength. It is in times of calmness and harmony that the mind, body and soul come together in unison to help you live life to its best.

Meditation gives you the required serenity of mind and a clear focus on your goal. Meanwhile, affirmations lend an air of positivity and determination to your thoughts. Learn to combine the power of meditations and affirmations to give you unparalleled peace and tranquility in life.

The Technique

Using affirmations while meditating is all about doing the exercise with a single-minded focus. To begin with, list down your feelings and observations as you meditate.

For instance, you might feel that slowly you are letting go of your tensions and feelings of hatred with each breath. In such a situation, you can simply use contrasting words for your affirmations.

Speak these words with each breath:

I let go of my stress (as you inhale)... *I am relaxed* (as you exhale).

I am not sad... I am happier.

The way to make affirmations and meditations work together is to create unison between your breath and the statement or affirmation. Learn to voice what you do not like as you inhale. Speak the positive and powerful affirmations when you exhale, as in the above examples.

Distractions and Directions

When you sit down to meditate, it is natural for your mind to wander off and get distracted. As you relax, your mind fills with thoughts that need to be controlled. Using positive affirmations as you meditate helps you ward off these distractions and keeps your focus intact.

Interestingly, once you learn how to meditate with affirmations, you will realize how you can use them to steer the direction of your meditating efforts. Your thoughts and affirmations will eventually begin to guide your mind in meditation. Take the example of following affirmations:

I feel more positive as I meditate.

I am feeling happier and more in control now.

I will mediate every day to relieve my stress.

The Core Logic

Here, the core logic lies in the way your mind works. An individual has the power to divert the energies of his mind in whichever direction he desires. You can easily use the power of positive statements to empower your process of meditation even more. Learn to manifest your will to be happy and relaxed. This way, you will help with determining the right outcome of your meditating efforts.

Chapter 9
Five-Step
Action Plan to
Your Vision

The simplest things are often less understood in life. Isn't it ironic that we keep complicating the logic of life, when the secret lies in simplicity?

The easiest route to happiness and success in life is simply doing the job at hand in the best possible way. Take good care of your family. Do your job with sincerity and had work. If you do not have a job, look for one with the best of your efforts.

Whatever your vision in life may be, make a sound action plan to get where you want.

Here are five easy steps for you to draw your own effective, result-oriented action plan in life.

The 5-Step Action Plan

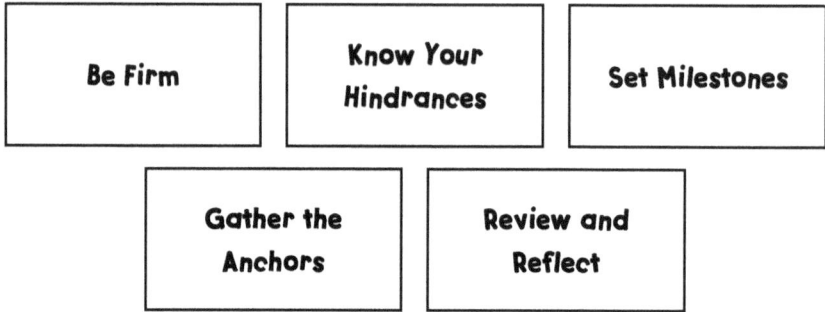

Be Firm	**Know Your Hindrances**	**Set Milestones**

Gather the Anchors	**Review and Reflect**

Step 1: Be Firm of Your Goal

Take your time in forming your vision. Once you know what you want, do not deviate from your objectives. You might face self-doubt and distractions on the way, but be firm of your vision to be able to forge ahead.

You might want to write a book. As you write on, you might start having doubts about how well you are writing or whether it will pay off to write a book. Remember that you can only know the actual outcome once you have finished the work.

So, take one of the goals that you have already written or set a new goal. Whatever this goal is, please make sure that you are writing **SMART** goals.

Here's some space to write your goals:

Goal # 1

S - _____

M - _____

A - _____

R- _____

T - _____

Goal # 2

S - _____

M - _____

A - _____

R- _____

T - _____

Goal # 3

S - _____

M - _____

A - _____

R- _____

T - _____

Step 2: Know Your Hindrances

Life happens to us all and it is important to know the difference between a hindrance and an emergency. They are not the same thing so it is important to take notice of the factors that could slow your progress. Examine your circumstances carefully, and be prepared for unforeseen circumstances.

For instance, if you work from home, leave enough time for family emergencies, which could be taxing for both your time and financial resources.

Ask yourself:

1. **Am I aware of what is preventing me from moving forward in my life?**

   It is important to identify your personal obstacles, so that you can begin removing them.

2. **Am I disciplined enough to create a path for myself in the world?**

   Discipline is one of the most important traits of powerful people. Be sure to practice it in your daily life.

3. **Am I receiving enough inspiration from my environment to nurture my creativity?**

   If the answer is no, change something! Even the smallest change can make a difference. Spend more time with loved ones, or meet someone new. Get a pet, or at least a new plant. Write down how you feel about the new experiences.

4. **Am I organized well enough to meet all my major and minor goals?**

   Being organized is crucial for success. We'll cover this question in our next step.

Step 3: Set Your Milestones

Make a timetable for yourself and be strict with your milestones. Divide the tasks into smaller deadlines and try to achieve each mini-goal. This will speed up your progress, and it will also reduce the scope of errors as you move along.

Let's say you're a writer, and you want to write a novel. It can be any genre you like, but for now, let's say it's a romance novel. To make matters worse, your publisher wants you to finish the first draft in only six weeks!

Writing a novel is difficult. You might have an abundant imagination, bursting with creativity. This is great. But, it might make the writing process longer if you don't keep it in check by using milestones.

Here's are some milestones you might set for yourself for the first two weeks in this example.

	Word count goal	Minor goals
Week 1		
Monday	2000 words	Quick story outline; First chapter: Create a hook and introduce the main characters.
Tuesday	2000 words	Show how great the characters function together, but also show what prevents them from realizing that. Have them interact with other characters to flesh them out. Show how similar, yet different they are.
Wednesday	2000 words	
Thursday	2000 words	
Friday	2000 words	
Saturday	Free time/Rest	Enjoy a day off!
Sunday	Review, Outline	Review what you wrote the week before and think about how the characters could proceed from there. Get ready to start Week 2 and write another 10000 words!

Week 2		
Monday	2000 words	Have the character spend more time together and show how they change through interacting with each other. In this phase, they start realizing that they like each other.
Tuesday	2000 words	
Wednesday	2000 words	Crisis! The characters are faced with an obstacle in their relationship. Show how it affects them. Show what they do to overcome the new difficulties.
Thursday	2000 words	
Friday	2000 words	Approaching the midpoint: the calm before the storm. Their relationship becomes stronger, but they're not yet ready to devote themselves to each other.
Saturday		Rest. You've earned it!
Sunday	Review, Outline	Review what you wrote the week before and think about how the characters could proceed from there. Get ready to start Week 3 and write another 10000 words!

Notice how the major goal of completing a novel in six weeks is broken into smaller, achievable goals, complete with a description of what you need to do in order to achieve them, and some time to rest, too!

Step 4: Gather Your Anchors

This is a very important step. You need anchors, which are individuals that are in your life to help you.

Mainly, these are your parents, siblings, close friends, teachers, inspirational figures, guides and other people that make a difference in your life. They ground you, provide support and believe in you. They make you feel safe, so you can settle down and start your own growth.

> **Example:** In our lives, we meet many people, and make them our friends. Some of those friendships can last a lifetime. Then there are those with whom you sometimes talk, but then you don't hear from them in months or years.

The most important are those that support you, not when you're at your lowest, but when you make a conscious decision to improve. Those who grip your hand tight and don't let you fall back down into the bad habits of the past.

Develop a strong support system around you. Know your strengths and put them to best use. Know what brings out the best in you.

For some individuals, exercise and music are therapeutic. These actually help in enhancing the overall levels of efficiency. Know what works for you and use it to the maximum.

Step 5: Review Your Progress

It helps to review your progress as you move along. Take a second to look back, and give yourself a pat on the back. You will be surprised at how well self-motivation works to help you achieve your goals.

Self-Reflection: What's Your Take on the Five-Action Plan?

1. What did you learn or accomplish using the five-action plan? Please be specific.

_____

_____

_____

_____

_____

_____

_____

_____

_____

_____

_____

_____

_____

_____

Chapter 10
Removing the Ego and Stepping Out of Faith

History is witness to the fact that the small misconceptions of human nature have always led to big consequences, even disasters. The biggest man-made tragedies have been the outcome of trivial but destructive human traits.

The Ego Trap

Ego and self-pride are perhaps the most difficult parts of human nature to overcome. When the heart is clouded with ego, the mind loses its power to distinguish between the right and wrong. It loses its focus on the goal, and eventually, the ability to perform.

Let us take a closer look at what this tendency is all about. Ego is a false sense of supreme self-worth, at the cost of everyone else around. While self-worth and self-esteem are positive traits, they become negative when we begin to think of ourselves and our decisions as superior to others around us.

Contrary to what we might think, it is faith and sincerity that win, not the false ego and high self-worth.

Faith – the Choice to Make

Self-confidence is required to reach our goals in life. Unfortunately, this confidence becomes a curse if it turns into a sense of superiority or inflated ego.

So, what is the ideal way to success, you may ask.

Are you ready for this?

It is in fact a simple, but often misunderstood, two-step process!

The right way to proceed towards your goal is to have an unshakeable, immense faith in your own ability. Without ever comparing yourself to others, just evaluate your performance with your own past record. Have faith that you can make the life you want to without getting into any shallow comparisons.

The Valuable Second Step

Once you learn how to get rid of your ego issues, you will gradually begin to develop faith in the ways of the Spirit. In our sense of supremacy, we often tend to overlook the power of the Spirit and begin to question His ways of working.

Instead, we ought to have faith that He has planned everything to the minutest detail and that He has his own ways of working with this world.

Human traits have the ability to make or break the world. Blessed are those who are able to rise above the evils of ego, hatred and jealousy. In fact, at times, simply being human is all that is required to survive happily in this world.

Chapter 11
Let Your Actions Speak

There is a unique contrast present in our universe. The prettiest of flowers bloom overnight and the calmest of seas carry the biggest storms. The law of nature dictates a major wave of mismatch between the cause and effect.

Human behavior, relationships and interactions are governed by the same rule. Often, the couples having maximum PDA or public display of affection have the weakest of relationships. After all, the heaviest of clouds seldom thunder before they shower!

So, in this chapter, we are going to focus on learning how to lead with humility, as that is how you are able to let your actions speak.

Leading with Humility – the Right Way

Let's start with a positive example.

There was once a man who worked in a company of 125 employees. All of them had different designations. Our man in question had CEO/Founder on the signboard just outside his cabin. In each of his conversations or public addresses, all you could hear was 'with' and never 'for'.

"I work with 125 employees" instead of "125 employees work for me."

A single man never made an army. After all, it takes a whole swarm of bees to build a hive.

Humility, a Virtue

A virtue is something that adds to the quality of life, both yours and of those around you.

Leadership is such a trait that can single-handedly revolutionize the lives of scores of people together.

Here's why leading with humility is the best way to create and nurture a winning team.

Humility Keeps Your Vision Clear

Humility does not dilute your vision or focus on the goal. You keep your attention on achieving your milestones instead of having to prove your supremacy.

Humble people are capable of leading very simple and fulfilling lives because they do not have the urge to show their dominance.

Humility Helps You Capitalize

It is a leader's responsibility to utilize the potential of each member of his team to the fullest. If you divert your energies towards a false sense of superiority, you will not be able to identify the strengths and weaknesses of those around you. Unless you do this, you will never be able to bring your team's potential to the maximum.

Humility Makes it Easier to Re-Plan

As meticulous as you might be, pitfalls, errors and disasters will always be there. When you work as a team and do not have any air of superiority around you, it becomes easier to re-plan and recover from your mistakes.

What's more, you can even bring in your colleagues and those who work with you to plan, think and take decisions. That way, everyone will feel equally responsible for the task at hand, which will eventually show in the results. In fact, it is much easier to win your team's confidence when you are one of them and not the one above.

Leadership is all about understanding your team, along with all of its subtle shades. With a firm vision on your goal and a humble attitude, you can easily forge ahead to achieve your pre-set goals.

Purity of Intentions – How Gratitude is at the Heart of Taking Action

Every stage of life is full of unexpected bounties and unforeseen adversaries. While you can sometimes hardly do anything about some of the negative situations that happen in your life, there is actually a lot that you can do with the favorable ones, beginning with genuine gratitude.

It takes a warm heart and an earnest soul to see the good fortune we have in life. Contrary to what you might think, lack of acknowledgement of what we have actually reduces the impact of our good fortune.

As nothing succeeds like success, positivity and gratitude bring not only good luck, but also the factors that enable success in future life.

The True Royalty

Royal are those who have the bliss of acknowledgement.

It is quite fascinating to realize just how gratitude is close to royalty. The royalty is a very limited group within the whole human race. In the same line, the blessed individuals knowing the art of gratitude are a handful few.

Here's how (and why) you should adopt this beautiful principle to make your life all the more livable.

The Feel-Good Factor

How many times have you looked back on your day and felt good about your achievements? Have you ever given yourself a pat on the back for a task well achieved? Well, gratitude is just that!

When we acknowledge what we have and are thankful for it, we open the doors for newer possibilities and opportunities. After all, have you ever heard of a cool breeze flowing in through closed windows?

Fill your heart with gratitude and watch your fortune change.

The Superiority Complex

Have you ever wondered about what it is that keeps you from feeling thankful?

The most common notion is that we probably deserve what we have. Have you ever realized that destiny could have favored you and given you a bit more than you actually deserved?

Since we really do not know what might be in store for us, it is always better for you to be thankful for whatever you have. For all we know, things could have been worse.

Little blessings can go a long way in life. Gratitude falls in the same class of ethical behavior as sincerity and truthfulness. Such virtues make your life more worthwhile and lend an air of positivity to your existence on a whole.

Learn to count each small blessing in your life, and be thankful for them, to have a happier tomorrow.

Words – The Gateway

The Spirit made this world to be moved only by action. If you look at it closely, the whole scenario in this cosmos follows a clear logical sequence.

The whole process starts with a simple thought, idea or an impulse.

For instance, you might have an idea to take up some DIY project at home. This is where the idea sprouts and might die if you do not hold on to it.

To help your thought grow, you need to think about it and put it into concrete words.

However, all the moments until now go waste if you fail to graduate to the next step, which is translating your words into meaningful, constructive action.

Do you see how this relates to vision boards?

By using vision boards, you create a bridge between your thoughts and their result in the world, helping yourself with the ultimate tool of motivation!

The World Today

Hypocrisy is the saddest thing in the modern world. From political heads to religious gurus and motivational speakers, to even spiritual leaders, all seem to be voicing things and principles they hardly follow. Shockingly enough, those who preach seem to be just doing the opposite of what they say.

It is for these reasons that laying more stress on actions is critical.

Read on for a set of handy rules and tips that will help you do just that.

The Top 5 Action Points

So, how do you make your actions speak louder than words? Follow our top five tips to make it work:

Top Five Tips

Think in a concrete and coherent manner before you speak.

Never over-commit. Only promise as much as you can deliver.

Always strive to be relevant and focused in your thoughts.

Keep small, achievable goals instead of long-term objectives.

Never try to impress with words.

Remember, to those that matter, your actions would be enough to convey what you mean. Just work to keep your thoughts and ideas clean, because your actions begin there.

Chapter 12
The Conclusion

Congratulations!

You learned everything there is to know about living your life to the fullest by using the simple logic that is weaved in the very fabric of the Universe. You unlocked the secret to a happier, more fulfilled life.

Throughout this book, we showed you the power of vision boards. We explained how and why they work, and how you can use them to achieve your dreams and goals.

We talked about how everything begins with a dream, and how making firm, concrete, SMART goals helps you follow the path towards accomplishing your objectives.

We showed you how to take your first steps to positive intentions by choosing your surroundings carefully.

You now know how to use belief systems as lighthouses that will guide you on your spiritual and professional journey, illuminating the path ahead.

You discovered why visualization is important, and how to prevent distractions when it comes to visualizing your objectives. You also learned of the two types of workers: the Novice and the Amateur.

We showed you how to use meditation and mindfulness as the ultimate tools in your life. You learned about some of the types of meditation, and how to start practicing them.

You learned about affirmations, and you know now how to use them to anchor the positivity to your life. We gave you tips on affirmations that work, and will help you bring out the best from life.

We advised you on how to use a 5-step plan to achieve your vision. We showed you how to set achievable milestones in order to defeat any obstacle that comes your way.

We showed you the nature of ego, and the importance of faith.

Most importantly, you learned how to take action and grab the life with your own two hands, by utilizing your greatest assets: humility and gratitude.

And now there's only one thing left.

Go forward in your journey, dear reader, and don't look back.

Walk with the Spirit and achieve your dreams.

Where to Go From Here

You can check out the Alise Spiritual Healing & Wellness Center to see how to schedule an intuitive reading, life coaching session, or to just hang out and learn what we are all about. Our website is the following: www.alisehealingcenter.com.

Looking for a guest speaker? Please go the Alise Spiritual Healing & Wellness Center site to invite Alise to speak.

Should you have questions or comments for us, suggestions for future material, or tips, feel free to email us at support@alisehealingcenter.com.

About the Author

ALISE Spiritual Healing & Wellness Center
Helping People Become Their Personal Best

We take pride in helping others believe in themselves and go far. As a Not For Profit, Alise Spiritual Healing & Wellness Center's mission is to educate, guide, heal, and empower every individual to become his or her personal best to live a balanced life in body, mind, and spirit. We believe strongly that we are here to help provide spiritual education, guidance, healing, and transformation to help enable people to create positive and lasting changes that will benefit them on their life journey.

Alise Spiritual Healing & Wellness Center is dedicated to providing the best spiritual guidance and upholding the ethics of a wellness holistic practitioner healing practice.

We work with clients either face-to-face or online around the world. For more information, visit www.alisehealingcenter.com.

Notes

Notes

Notes

Notes

Notes

Notes

Notes

Notes

Notes

Notes

Notes

Notes

Notes

Notes

Notes

Notes

Notes

Notes

Notes

Notes

www.ingramcontent.com/pod-product-compliance
Lightning Source LLC
Chambersburg PA
CBHW070537030426
42337CB00016B/2239